Beautiful

Outliers

Catherine Anabel White

Design: Margo Garrigues
Editors: John Tyler White, Misty Gallo

Printed in the United States of America

ISBN-13: 978-0-578-63036-6

Dedication

To my two heroes: John Tyler and Oliver Graham White. You both are the reason and the inspiration for this book and every one that follows.

Contents

Part Four: Self Care

Part Five: Anonymity

Part Six: Comparison

Part Seven: Culture

01

Intro to Motherhood

"Therefore welcome one another as Christ has welcomed you,
for the glory of God." – ROMANS 15:7

The welcoming into motherhood is an abrupt one, the sort of welcoming that skips the hugs and kisses. Not waiting for your "come on in," it heads straight for your parked car, where you'll strap in your newborn for the very first time. The welcome to motherhood is a silent one, despite the frequent cries from your newborn ushering in the first of many sleep-deprived nights. You thought nine months was enough mental preparation...

You thought.

Welcome to motherhood, a worldwide community of approximately 2 billion.

Welcome to motherhood, this incredible, frazzling, growing, challenging, lifelong season that is often under-appreciated by culture, but immensely celebrated and cherished by our Heavenly Father. He is calling us to understand and learn from this new role under His perspective, to embrace it with His strength and grace as we rise up in culture with our voices and our giftings.

We can't fully live out His calling if we respond out of fear, control, or isolation, which means as we enter into motherhood, we must choose contentment over complaining and thanksgiving over impatience. We must choose to live in the season we're in, as we trust and listen to His voice.

Welcome to motherhood, dear fellow mother. Welcome to the challenges and joys, the valleys and mountains, the newness and growth. It's a lifelong journey, one that's just begun, but the calling is great.

Enter this new role in dialogue with Him. Hear Him say, "You are seen, you are loved, and I am so proud of you, daughter."

How's it going, mama? As you enter into motherhood, where are you physically, mentally, spiritually, emotionally? What's He speaking to you about this season?

Part One

Darkness to Light

02

Challenge: Pesky Perversions

"For as he thinks in his heart, so is he." – PROVERBS 23:7 NKJV

Little, pesky thoughts nag and nag at the new mom.

They whisper,

You're not equipped for this role.

To be a good, caring mom, you need to worry about your baby often.

You're not as good a mom as she is.

You're making no impact. Your life isn't significant.

You need to be in control.

Your baby's not developing like he/she should.

You're all alone.

We'll expose and eradicate these lies throughout the month, but first we must recognize how these lies (among others offered to us) will produce death and discouragement if we meditate on them.

Like Joyce Meyer says, we must think about what we think about.

"We can't just hope we will think good thoughts. We have to actively seek them. We have to think purposely, not passively. A passive mind is a dangerous thing; passive people want good things to happen to them, but they just wait around to see what will happen. They do nothing to contribute to a positive result in their lives. The devil wants us to be passive because then he can work his plan without any opposition from us. But the Bible tells us to resist the devil, and he will flee. Be an active person who is always working with God toward the result that you desire to see in your life."[1]

We, as new moms, must be on guard with what we think throughout the day. We will be offered lies that tell us we aren't doing a good job, we're insignificant, or we're going crazy. Instead of passively accepting those thoughts as true, we must fight with His Word, reflecting and meditating on what He says about us.

We may feel exhausted. We may even feel defeated. And the enemy may tell us that we are. But that's when we remind ourselves, "*The joy of the Lord is my strength*," and, "*We are more than conquerors through Him who loves us*" (Neh. 8.10; Rom. 8.37).

Reflect on what lies are being offered to you right now. What does the Lord say about you? Write out a Scripture verse that speaks truth into the situation.

03

Lie: I'm The Only One

"Am I a God at hand. declares the Lord. and not a God far away? Can a man hide himself in secret places so that I cannot see him? declares the Lord. Do I not fill heaven and earth? declares the Lord." – JEREMIAH 23:23-24

"I'm the only one."

Maybe you're a superwoman and haven't experienced this lie, but I sure have.

The 1am, 4am, then 6am feeds. The 3am cry of, "I misplaced my paci, someone come save me." The 3:15am, "my diaper's full." Ignore. Then 3:25, "my swaddle's wet now." Ughhh. By 3:30 you're back in bed but waiting for the next wake-up cry, which will probably be for a feeding or a holding or something. All the while we think, "I'm the only one."

The night lingers and lingers and we feel alone. We forget to imagine the hundreds of thousands (probably millions) of other mothers breastfeeding with us in that moment.

And for the single mom especially, this will lie press and taunt saying, "you're really the only one."

Of course, we know all those frequently posted verses like, "He will never leave or forsake you." Or, "I am with you always." Yet, we don't meditate on or let those verses saturate deep within us. When pangs of loneliness hit, we often repeat the lie and live in our feelings rather than reflect on the truth of His Word.

We hear our babies cry, we watch our husbands leave for work each morning without us, we wake up alone and think: motherhood is lonely. I'm all alone.

You might be physically alone with your baby, but do not forget the significance of the Lord's presence being with you wherever you are. He's rocking the baby with you. He's right beside you in the sleepless nights, the holed-up days. We have a present God who cares about us and our baby. He knew exactly how these first days, first weeks, and first months of motherhood would go.

He allows us to experience these moments alone so that we might press into His presence. There's no greater opportunity to dialogue with Him than now. We've got the time for it. We've got the need for it.

Instead of meditating on, "I'm all alone," let's ask the Lord to reveal more of Himself to us. Let's watch Him disclose His character, His voice, and His love through these quiet, hidden days with our little ones.

May we pause and enjoy this friendship with our Savior and Father. And may we pray for all the other moms across the globe experiencing the same things we are, as we mother alongside one another and remind each other that we're not alone in this. We have the Lord and we have each other.

Ask the Lord for a deeper awareness of His presence today.
Use the moments where you feel "alone" to build a friendship
with your Heavenly Father.

04

Joy: That Ever-Brilliant Light

"But the Lord will be your everlasting light.
and your God will be your glory." – ISAIAH 60:19B

It's the holiday season, and that means Christmas lights upon Christmas lights upon Christmas lights. Icicle lights, gingerbread lights, classic lights. They're everywhere, and Graham adores it.

My husband told me about a public prayer he gave this morning where he reflected on the fact that, despite winter's naturally shortening and darkening days, accidentally or on purpose, our culture has taken to remembering the coming of Christ with light.

In our literal darkest days, there are still lights strung around trees. Shouldn't that be symbolic of our spiritual life? That in the dark moments, amidst the unforgiving brutality of a cold wind, unkind words, or harsh realities, the peace of God's fulfilled promises and the hope of those yet to be demand recognition. They are the light that, like Graham, we can't help but look at, mesmerized and infatuated with their aura.

We wonder how to free ourselves from the lies of the enemy, how to walk through the darkest hours where we feel alone, out of control, or like a failing mama.

Here's how: Just look around you. See the promises God has made and kept and believe He will continue to keep them.

The Word of God, the work of God, and the hope of God -- that's everlasting light; light that is ever present, ever brilliant.

The Lord reveals Himself in endless ways and countless places. He's everywhere we go, just like the Christmas lights dangling and shining in our neighborhoods and shopping malls.

Every time Graham starts to cry, we'll carry him straight to a Christmas tree where he stares at the lights for what feels like hours.

Perhaps we can all learn from my little one. When we feel overwhelmed as moms, when we start to cry in the darkness, let's walk ourselves to His light. Let's let the truth of His Word illuminate and eliminate our worries.

Graham's facial expression says, "It's okay," as he stares at each bulb.

And, dear mama, it will be.

Carry around a notecard with Isaiah 60:19b today.
As you notice physical lights around you, pull out that notecard
and meditate on the verse.

05

Karen Shackelford

THE OVERCOMER

"For freedom Christ has set us free; stand firm therefore, and do not submit again to a yoke of slavery." – GALATIANS 5:1

Meet Karen Shackelford.

My mom.

The person who taught me how to fight back against elementary school bullies with love and kindness. The constant supporter, prayer warrior, and encourager amidst my worst days.

She's taught me the importance of how to think, and how to experience freedom from the lies of the enemy by shifting my thoughts to align with His.

Fight lies with truth. His Word.

Remember your freedom.

Say no to negativity.

Never give up.

Meditate on what He says about you instead of what you think or feel about yourself.

I learned these things by watching her overcome stage 3 breast cancer with sixteen rounds of chemo, thirty-five rounds of radiation, and nine major surgeries. And, seven years later, a thyroid crash where her heartbeat averaged almost two hundred beats a minute. I heard about the nine pound tumor in her uterus at twenty-one, the possibility of never having kids or being high risk. She overcame that with my two brothers and me, all C-section babies.

She's used her victories to free others. I've seen countless women come up and ask my mom to mentor someone else going through cancer.

I've listened to her encouragement as she shared her own victorious testimony. I watched her fast and pray with suffering women. I also saw her start her own ministry for cancer patients called Kare-N-for-Cancer, where individuals and families sponsored Christmas for patients and their families who couldn't manage it themselves.

Over the past few years, she's led almost ten different Bible studies on Joyce Meyer's *Battlefield of the Mind*, ranging from high school students to grandmas.

Let her testimony encourage you and tell you that your story, your trials, your victories have impact. They hold significant weight in the Kingdom.

Free mamas free mamas.

Let's free ourselves of the lies that entangle us, not just for our own sake and that our families, but also for all the other mamas and families we can impact through our freedom.

You are not chained or defined by your circumstances. Just look at my mom. She didn't defer hope. Yes, she was realistic about her circumstances and knew she'd have to walk through chemo, radiation, etc. But she didn't back down or release her mind to every wayward thought. No tumor, cancer, or thyroid issues could steal her hope or joy for the destiny the Lord had and still has for her.

The Lord is using these formulating moments in our lives to reach other moms who may be walking through the same things we are.

Don't give up. Keep fighting.

Someone out there needs the hope of your testimony.

Spend a few moments today reflecting on your testimony. What has the Lord brought you through? Where have you experienced victory? Consider who might benefit from you sharing your testimony this week.

Part Two

New Territories

06

Challenge: Not So Smooth Sailin'

"He made the storm be still, and the waves of the sea were hushed."
– PSALM 107:29

Nothing prepares you for motherhood as much as being thrown into motherhood itself.

That is what it feels like.

Thrown.

Flung.

Tossed.

A frenetic twist into baby 101. At least, that's how it began for me.
How do I breastfeed? Am I the only one who hates pumping? Why is he making those weird noises in his sleep? He feels hot. He feels cold. He's sweating. He's crying.

The newness of this season creates a hyper-awareness as we try to play catch-up with what we feel like we should know, but in fact do not.

I mean, I learned the hard way that grocery shopping with an infant is no easy feat. Use the stroller as a cart? Sure, goodluck fitting a week's worth of items at its floorboard. Baby carrier? No problem, it'll fit in the cart perfectly, leaving you room for about one item. Backpack for baby? This wound up working for me, except on the days he felt like screaming in protest at such confinement.

We're navigating new waters here, mama. And those waters aren't always smooth sailing like Instagram projects. The shifting winds and waves this season blows in demand we earn our sea-legs.

But this is the beauty of such new, befuddling territories. The Lord isn't asking us for absolute perfection and omniscience, He's got that covered. He is asking for our obedience to learn the things He wants us to learn in this season. We know that He'll never leave or forsake us, which means we can boldly approach the choppy parenting waters with confidence that He'll pull through and show us how to proceed. The same Spirit living in the One who calmed the storms, and in Peter who walked on water, lives in you. Watch the storm still and waves hush at His touch.

Remember that while the enemy wants to use your inexperience to intimidate, overwhelm, and exhaust you, the Lord wants to use this as an opportunity to show you His Lordship over all as you commit to trusting His leadership and ability.

Enter these new motherhood gates with thanksgiving. Lift up your sails and enjoy this new adventure that awaits, amidst high, foreign waters.

> *What storms are you facing as you enter motherhood? Finances?*
> *Recovery from delivery? Mental stamina? Submit your storm to*
> *the Lord today, and watch Him move.*

07

Lie: I'm Not Equipped

"That the man of God may be complete, equipped for every good work."
– 2 TIMOTHY 3:17

It's week two, and I decide Graham and I could use a bit of fresh air. We drive half a mile to this cute, quaint little park with tall, looming trees and brilliant sunlight.

I grab the folded stroller out of the car, realizing this is the first time I'm using this thing....realizing I've never used a stroller before...realizing my lack of knowledge on how to open the contraption.

I mess with it for about 5 minutes, starting to feel embarrassed at stares from park walkers. I finally give up, resorting to YouTube. After about 7 videos, I've come to learn that there's a gray side button you gently tug till you hear a *click. Voila, you've got yourself an unfolded stroller.

It only took me 30 minutes.

"You're not equipped."

The lie lingered our entire stroller ride. Maybe I'm not cut out for this. Am I not mom material? Why's it so hard for me when everyone else makes it look so easy?

That lie resurfaces often, when Graham cries inconsolably and refuses to be held. Or while bathing when his face slips from our grip and submerges beneath the water. Or after discovering an infected fingernail. Or how after a month there's still the infected fingernail.

During new seasons, the enemy wants to tell us we're not qualified. That motherhood doesn't suit us. We don't belong in this role. He'll drive us into insecurity and fear and isolation, as we hide in shame what we believe are our fatal mistakes.

But the Lord says, before you even were, you're qualified. I've called you — to this family, this baby, this season.

Feel the freedom to make mistakes and learn more intimately His grace and redemption. To the same extent man is responsible, God is both sovereign and good. And He declares us free.

His love is strong. It carries us through these moments larger than ourselves and says, "You're equipped because you've got me. If I'm for you, who's against you?"

He's called you to this role, and His Spirit lives within you to equip you in your calling as a mother. Listen to His voice and follow His guidance into all truth. Remember not to focus on how you feel about yourself, but on what He says about you: "What do you mean you're not equipped? I'm the Divine Equipper."

Think about an area where you feel unequipped. Reflect on the resources the Lord's given you to be victorious in that area.

26

08

Joy: Ordinary Miracles

"Know that the Lord, he is God!" – PSALM 100:3

Oh, the sweet surprises of watching a newborn blossom into his very own self.

The first smile, the cute coos, the warm snuggles.

Sure, this trek into motherhood has certainly posed its challenges, with more forecasted for the future.

But soak in the miracle of the season. Bask in this tiny human with a profound calling. Enjoy the fruits of partaking in the Lord's work. Claim a front row seat to your baby's growth and firsts.

The greatest gift we can give our little ones is our presence, our eyes, our ears, our healthy selves. When we do so, we will witness our children making memories of us and the world around them.

I'm delighted by Graham's fascination with warm baths, the way his mouth opens in absolute wonder at scalp rubs and gentle tickles on his belly. I admire his admiration for a big, bright world full of falling leaves and loud cars and catchy melodies.

Even amidst the slowest of days, I watch him watching the world with such innocence and joy, the way we all should. He reminds me to bask in the beauty surrounding us, beauty awaiting our attention and praise, as if we're witnessing its magic for the first time.

Certainly, there's an overabundant supply of newness in motherhood. However, in spite of all this newness, "Know that the Lord, he is God!" He's got this, mama. He's got the consistency and foundation you need in this season. He'll cover the hard stuff, if you'll simply let Him.

And remind yourself during these ever-changing days: His mercies are the same. His kindness is the same. His grace continues like a steady stream. You are certainly called to be a mom, to love well, to live these days sacrificially for your infant who needs you.

But release these bewildering, new, confusing moments to Him, who happens to have all the answers. He is our source for everything. And remember to enter into the little and large joys offered as a new mom. Record the smiles, the finger-holds, the wiggles.

Something, someone, is forming before your eyes. Will you cherish the miracle you're witnessing?

Record the little nuances of your little one.
What strengths do you already see in him/her?

09

Lot's Wife

HINDSIGHT HAZARDS

"But Lot's wife, behind him, looked back, and she became a pillar of salt." –
GENESIS 19:26

Meet Lot's wife, who had men arrive at her family's home in Sodom urging them to leave.

Lot's wife, who heard how the outcry against the city's people was so great, the Lord sent men to destroy it with sulfur and fire.

Lot's wife, who was told, "Escape for your life. Do not look back or stop anywhere in the valley" (v. 17).

Lot's wife, who looked back anyway.

A pillar of salt.

This is a warning for us new moms. The past life, the days we could live somewhat irresponsibly for ourselves, are over. The Lord is bringing us into a new place, into a better land with a new community.

Jesus tells us to remember Lot's wife, how "whoever seeks to preserve his life will lose it, but whoever loses his life will keep it" (Luke 17.33).

Do not become so attached to your old, pre-baby life that you regret the things you've lost and forget the joy of this new season.

Lot's wife neglected to joyfully leave Sodom and hurry to the new place the Lord called her and her family.

Might we learn from her mistake, and cheerfully leave our past behind, hastening to where He calls us. These new territories are foreign and unknown, but He's already gone before us and prepared wonderful and glorious things -- if we will be obedient to move forward, without looking back.

What's hindering you from hastening to where He's calling you?
What things in the past do you need to let go of today?

Part Three

Keeping Peace

10

Challenge: Process to Peace

"And let the peace of Christ rule in your hearts..." – COLOSSIANS 3:15

Tomorrow marks 2 months with the wide eyed, gummy smile of a son who somehow intertwines a sweet disposition with bold ferocity.

Life changes faster than a blink, or should I now say faster than a diaper change?

If motherhood has taught me anything, it's how to be flexible. Change demands adaptivity and our willingness to be stretched and pulled in all the most uncomfortable places. It offers us the opportunity to depend on God more than ever, because we can't even think of a possible solution to any given problem. Two months of off-and-on napping can certainly throw a crook in our thinking.

Let's face it - we make plans. We schedule. We Google. But there are still things, namely our baby and when he cries, completely out of our control. We try to rationalize it all. He's crying "because he's tired," "because he's hungry," "because he's overstimulated," "because he's sick," etc. Sure, oftentimes those things are true. But sometimes he cries without reason or permission.

I'm here to encourage the momma comparing herself to the online schedules, general expectations, and various, exhausting articles concerning other babies the same age: don't. This experience, just like life, is hand-tailored to you and your baby. We have a creative Lord who likes us to be reminded of the fact that He is Lord. Not our schedules. Not our expectations.

Let go of the Google-driven fear that something is wrong with your baby because he's blinking earlier than most...

Deep breaths.

Might I encourage us as women to ask the Lord for His wisdom before Googling or WebMD-ing our questions? Won't He know? Doesn't He want this experience to bring you further into his arms, as he reminds you that while you have a child you still are a child?

Our babies need us to choose peace, the radical kind that puts the phone and monitor down for the night, relaxing in a peaceful sleep which says, "All is well. He is this baby's protector and provider."

And while the enemy uses fear as a snare to keep us from fully embracing this beautiful, miraculous season with our children, we have the opportunity to say no.

So say no. Make the steps necessary to live a life filled with peace, because our babies need it. And soak in these short long days as you watch your baby's personality form, body grow, and mind sharpen. Taste the sweetness of the season, the raspberries soaked in honey, the gumdrop grins of a healthy baby adored by a joy-filled mama. Its sweetness depends on our peace.

Reflect on whatever fears are hindering peace and joy amidst this season. Release them to the Lord. Spend today running to the Lord with your questions and concerns rather than Google.

11

Lie: Worrying is Part of the Job

"When I am afraid, I put my trust in you." – PSALM 56:3

"Worrying is part of the job."

I think this is perhaps one of the enemy's favorite lies he offers us moms, because fear kills delight. Instead of experiencing all the adventure and fun the Lord pours into this new role, the enemy would rather us feel insecure, with our minds fixated on the endless "what-if" possibilities.

We keep our babies in our rooms for months upon months out of fear of SIDS.

We stay holed up in our homes the first few months because we don't want our baby to catch any airborne germs. Or, we never take our baby anywhere out of fear they'll start crying and cause a "scene."

We overprotect in the name of caring. Certainly we ought to be cognizant of our newborn's capabilities and be careful to prevent things like sickness, overstimulation, etc.

But dear mama, do not forget the important fact that this baby is more His than yours. God has entrusted you with a life, certainly. But you also must trust Him with your baby. And that looks like watching for His cues for when it's appropriate to transition to the crib, leave home, or dine out as a family.

Remember, He asks for total trust in every area, including your baby's health and wellness. Let go of that tight grip on fear, for by parenting from fear we establish fear in our baby.

Let's show them in these early weeks and months what it looks like to trust Him boldly in all things, beginning with the people we love most.

Consider your fears and ponder whether they've been influenced by your parents. For example, are you afraid to try mayonnaise because your mom always told you it was nasty? (If so, you're in the same boat as both my husband and me). Pray over your fears and release them to the Lord. Ask Him what practical steps you need to take to trust Him with your little one today.

12

Joy: The Delight of Priority

"And a harvest of righteousness is sown in peace by those
who make peace." – JAMES 3:18

Graham's first Christmas tree is a North Carolina Fraser Fir, standing slightly above 7 feet. We picked it out among hundreds of other trees at North Pole Farms, and I couldn't help but laugh at Graham's gaping mouth and bulging eyes. He absolutely adores our fir tree, and his content demeanor was a wonderful surprise following the car ride of hysterical, blood-curdling crying on the way to pick it up.

The next hour home was a continuation of that piercing, heartbreaking cry. That is, until he calmed down enough to feed and fall asleep. He's now sleeping peacefully in the other room with both hands folded by his head and a warm swaddle to keep his toes warm. And I am undertaking the simple task of putting up Christmas decor...

This, dear mama, is what it looks like when we choose peace over anxiety. We keep driving the car to our destination despite wanting to turn home and toss our original idea out the window (although sometimes this is a necessary decision). We use trial and error to understand our baby's needs instead of rushing to the worst possible outcome and caving into full-throttle panic mode.

By choosing to think heaven-minded thoughts instead of negative-minded ones, we create an atmosphere of peace within our home that benefits our families. This doesn't mean external circumstances aren't ever challenging or hard, but it does mean choosing to have peace in our hearts in spite of those things.

Proverbs 31:27 says, "She looks well to the ways of her household and does not eat the bread of idleness."

We cannot tend to our household and its needs if we bite into the rotten apple of whatever lie the enemy offers. Fear and negative thoughts stilt growth and hinder productivity. They encourage us as moms to become fixated on whatever problem or worry we have, so much so that we neglect our other roles, such as being a wife, a daughter, an employee, etc.

Choosing peace means creating the space for us to nourish important needs in all aspects of our lives-- yes, even the ones outside of our babies.

It means setting up Christmas decor with your husband and falling asleep in his arms while watching a cheesy Hallmark movie.

It means grocery shopping and meal prepping and, dare I say, showering.

We have a significant influence on the atmosphere for our home, and our families need us to choose peace.

Choose peace, because not only you, but your little one will reap its benefits, even if he cries in the midst of it.

How can you choose peace today? Ask the Lord to reveal any opportunity. How will those around you benefit from this decision?

13

Robin Barlow

THE HEAVENLY THINKER

"For nothing will be impossible with God." – LUKE 1:37

Meet Robin Barlow.

A mentor, a role-model, a mother of four. I spent many lonely nights at her home during college, pondering things like my purpose or my relationship with the Lord. She always taught me, through her actions and words, the need to change my thinking and begin to partner with Heavenly thoughts over earthly ones.

I saw her turn worry into prayer and fasting. I witnessed consistent overcoming and impossible victories. In 2018, her husband was diagnosed with Chronic Lymphocytic Leukemia (CLL) and Richter's Transformation. MD Anderson had only witnessed 20 cases in the past 40 years, it was that rare.

In fact, the Leukemia Foundation explains how Richter's is considered a "serious complication of CLL and unfortunately is often fatal...it is advised that the person should seek recommended treatments, but also get their lives in order to prepare for any outcome."[1] The odds kept stacking against him, but instead of planning funeral arrangements, Robin spent her time fasting and praying. I never heard her speak one doubtful word into his situation. She chose to believe the impossible, and four months later they heard the impossible word: remission!

Even 17 years ago, when their third child was diagnosed with Aspergers and everyone deemed his future insignificant, she felt the Lord say, "Don't agree with that." God is the God of impossibilities. He roots for the underdog. Instead of meditating on doubt and unbelief, she decided to align herself with hope, which meant she wouldn't limit her son with her words.

It meant letting him fly from Bentonville, Arkansas, to Los Angeles to audition for a New York Film Academy when "the odds were against" a 19-year old with Aspergers. He got in, by the way.

It means letting him dream of marriage, of moving to Japan, of whatever else he aspires to.

The Lord says, "Give me time to work in that." Robin's response is always a posture of prayer, fasting, and thankfulness.

Let that be an example for you, the way it has been for me. Don't limit the Lord with your thoughts, or your baby with your words. Like Robin says, "you can't afford one thought in your mind that doesn't line up with heaven." Choose wisdom. Choose hope. Choose freedom.

"What you overcome Graham gets," she said. "When you overcome fear, when you don't live in it, Graham inherits that victory. He gets peace because you chose to live in peace."

Don't allow your inner life to turn into turmoil, because your house will, too.

Instead, let's ask the Lord: what do you think about this? How do we walk through this? How do we not fall into despair?

If we'll make space for Heaven to speak into our circumstances, our family will reap the fruits.

Where do you and your family need God to work?
Believe the impossible.

Reflection

READ LUKE 12:22-34

Amidst the hustle-and-bustle of motherhood, it's easy for us to skip these types of days. Reflection days.

We want the meat, the quick verse, the catchy phrase.

But times to pause and reflect are vital for our spiritual, physical, and emotional health. Even if it's for 5 minutes on your back patio overlooking 7-11, Firestone, and Johnson Cleaners (me right now). Or during your bath. Or while the main dish cooks in the oven.

Find the time. Pause. Breathe. Process. Reflect.

How am I doing? What are my needs today? Where have I seen God? What am I thankful for? What little miracles have I witnessed the past two weeks?

Ask yourself a question or two. Journal or ponder your response. Then, release your needs to the Lord. Give yourself over to a little gratefulness for all He's done for your family. After all, you've made it this far.

And if you're feeling anxious or antsy, read this section of Luke. He knows your needs. He will provide.

Part Four
Self Care

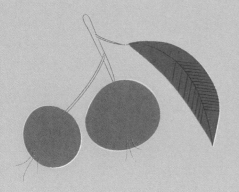

14

Challenge: The Prism of Productivity

"All who are skilled among you are to come and make everything the LORD has commanded." – EXODUS 35:10

I'm sitting on some rusty park bench, typing this while Graham lightly sleeps in his stroller.

He hasn't napped in over 5 hours, which means my hands have been full.

I think we all quickly learn as new moms our need to be flexible. Plans change because babies are fairly unpredictable. We can use that as an excuse to wait hand and foot on our babies, neglecting our own needs. Or we can learn the art of being creative with our time, like writing on iPhone notes during a random stroll.

While I had plans to write today, I didn't say, "At 12:28 pm I will write this devo."

I hadn't planned on strolling today. I didn't even know this park bench existed until now. But an inconsolable baby with his own agenda meant modifying.

We can adapt while still taking care of ourselves. We don't have to give up on the things we love, the things that refresh us, just because our days are unpredictable.

Your baby needs a happy, healthy you. He needs to see his mom make time for herself.

You're an example for how to create margin and cultivate the gifts entrusted to you, as you seize those pockets the Lord gives throughout a day to do what He's calling you to do instead of binge-watching Netflix or dialoguing in negative self-talk.

Make yourself a priority.

Your dreams and talents don't have to die when you have a baby. In fact, if we'll become more intentional with our time, we'll see that now more than ever is an opportunity to grow our giftings and challenge our capabilities. Even if it is for fifteen minutes on a park bench in between cries.

What do you need to make time for during these days? What talent is the Lord asking you to grow, and what steps do you need to take to make sure you do so?

15

Lie: My Baby's Falling Behind

"Are not two sparrows sold for a penny? And not one of them will fall to the ground apart from your Father. But even the hairs of your head are all numbered." – MATTHEW 10:29-30

"6 pounds!"

My mind reeled.

Six pounds. Graham came out almost three pounds lighter than what the doctor predicted. Yes, the nurse told me she was sure. Six pounds even, which put him in the 2nd percentile.

Initially, I didn't care what pound he was. He's out and that's all that matters, I thought.

But in those first few days of breastfeeding, this lie tried to establish itself:

"Your baby's falling behind."

You're not producing enough milk. He's not eating well.

Since it's not like I could measure how many ounces he got each feeding, I started feeling inadequate, like I was letting my baby down. He'd feed for 15 minutes, and I doubted whether that was enough. I was also trying to establish a schedule pretty early on, and I wondered whether that was a poor mom decision since he was so little.

Our first pediatrician appointment was just a few days after we got back from the hospital. I was warned about the likelihood of Graham losing weight since leaving the hospital. It's very common. However, he gained two ounces. Woo hoo! Small victories.

I celebrated that success until the next few feedings, when I felt the lies resurface.

You aren't producing enough. He's way behind all the other babies his age.

I've struggled against all the lies we discuss in this devo, but this particular one struck me the most.

The "you aren't producing enough" turned into, "you aren't enough."

It was at Graham's two week checkup that I learned the truth.

I was!

More than enough. Graham gained over a pound a week those first two weeks. And, at his 2 month checkup, he'd gained another 2 pounds, placing him in the 75th percentile for such rapid growth.

Now, maybe you don't struggle with "my baby's falling behind" in terms of breastfeeding.

Maybe it's the milestones. The fear that most babies are grabbing by now and she's not, or smiling and he's not, etc. There are certain instances where maybe we ought to look into those things, but more often than not, we become impatient and fearful that there aren't results (or that we're seeing the wrong ones). People ask if he's rolling over, and we begin worrying about why he hasn't. We ignore all the other milestones he does early, focusing on the negative.

Dear mama, while we are responsible for our babies, the Lord is responsible for their growth. He hasn't forgotten about your baby. He isn't confined to what a book or article says about when your baby will do x, y, and z. He's made your baby incredibly unique, with his or her very own personality. That personality happens to shine through in these early days.

As a parent, there are all sorts of seeds you want sown into your baby's life. There's no way you alone can sow them all. Sometimes it is enough to simply create good ground: to rest in the fact that you are watching, you are nourishing, you are bathing your child. Many times you do sow the seeds. Others, they're sown by unexpected people in God's time. You can wait on Him. Just because your baby is not taking a particular step forward yet does not mean they're taking a step back.

Enjoy watching your baby's development, but don't rush these days. Treasure these little hints and glimpses into who your baby is, and remind yourself that the Lord has a timeline, which might look different than your expectations.

Let's not limit God. Let's humble ourselves and give His mighty hand the ability to work (1 Pet. 5.6).

What are you doing to create "good ground"?
How is having a willingness to let your baby grow at
God's pace relevant to sowing seeds in peace?

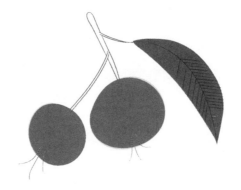

16

Joy: Moments to Fashion

"Do not neglect the gift you have." – 1 TIMOTHY 4:14

I was in the middle of graduate school, freelance writing opportunities, and applying for the White House Fellows program when I found out I was pregnant.

I finished my degree, but the latter two I sidelined for the ominous "future."

Besides the "When's your due date?" and "How are you feeling?" questions, I also received a lot of, "Will you go back to work? What will you do?"

I clung to the, "I'm not sure" mantra. Still am, I suppose.

Partway through the second trimester, though, my husband mentioned the idea of doing something creative during one of baby's nap-times each day. I planned on implementing that as soon as Graham arrived, however the first two weeks were such a whirlwind, I found myself napping, Netflixing, or calling my mom for advice instead.

With baby napping four times a day, I started getting in the groove of journaling, blogging, even sketching at least once a day. Even if it's only 20-30 minutes, that time rejuvenates and refreshes my soul. It relaxes and stimulates my mind in a way Netflix or a phone call can't.

And now here I am writing this devo, something I never thought I'd actually finish or publish.

I love how the Lord gives us these brief pauses in our day to separate from our little ones and pick up the crafts we love. He carves out the time for us to innovate and imagine, to stimulate our minds in a different way.

Bruce Garrabrandt said, "Creativity doesn't wait for that perfect moment. It fashions its own perfect moments out of ordinary ones."[1]

We've got plenty of ordinary moments to fashion, dear mama. It's time to roll up your sleeves and get your hands dirty, just not from a diaper this time.

What gift are you neglecting, what passion are you denying, what dream are you ignoring? Go after it with vigor, even if that looks like only 5-10 minutes a day of sharpening one skill or sketching 1 inch of a page. We still have our limitations as new moms, like our baby crying in the midst of her nap. There's certainly grace in the midst of our pursuits. But don't spend these days in passivity or self-pity, excusing yourself from where the Lord's calling you to create, design, impact.

Your identity is not in your baby, in your role as a mother, or in your family, though those are all wonderful things. Your identity is in Him, and it's time we ask Him what Heavenly work He's got planned for us today.

Spend 5-10 minutes today away from the to-do list, doing something creative that refreshes you.

17

Cheyenne Tuepker

THE ENDURER

"Count it all joy, my brothers, when you meet trials of various kinds"
– JAMES 1:2

Meet Cheyenne Tuepker.

A 25-year-old who, partway into her first year of marriage, enjoyed a delightful surprise at the announcement of her coming son, Titus Nash Tuepker.

Pregnancy presented some unprecedented challenges. First, there was the severe morning sickness, intruding on the peaceful rise of a quiet morning and lingering, unsolicited, late into the evenings. At around 16 weeks, Cheyenne was diagnosed with placenta previa, a rare complication (about one in two-hundred pregnancies) where the placenta is so low in the uterus the mother's cervix is either partially or entirely covered, sometimes causing extreme bleeding during pregnancy and labor. Thankfully, hers resolved itself early into her third trimester before delivery. She also overcame strep throat, a deep tissue infection on her leg, and a visit at 29 weeks to the emergency room in response to bleeding and regular contractions.

Titus came early, almost two months before his due date. First hellos and warm snuggles were cut short. He had to be taken from his new family and brought to the NICU, which would be his "home" for the following 23 days. Home looked like lots of wires— IV's, feeding tubes, etc. With Cheyenne's husband headed back to work, she stayed in the hospital by herself. If that wasn't hard enough, her visits with Titus were limited to one hour periods twice a day. Her baby's progress was constantly up in the air, often shifting between good and bad news.

One day, an unexpected encounter with an elderly lady visiting her very ill husband transformed Cheyenne's perspective on her circumstances.

"My journey with my baby in the NICU may be three steps forward and two steps back, but thank goodness we had steps to be taking forward," Cheyenne reflected.

The same afternoon, Cheyenne trekked to Wal-Mart and printed off photos for a scrapbook. She bought a journal, and began documenting the highs and lows of each day. Before she could actually articulate the fruit of her endeavor, Cheyenne began to feel the life that accompanied creativity in a situation where the enemy wanted to rob her family of both. Now, almost three months later, she continues to add photos and memories to this artistic compilation.

Dear mama, "count it all joy when you meet trials of various kinds" (James 1.2). If we will live by faith amidst our trials, if we will endure hardship in the form of extended hospital visits and feeding tubes and delayed progress, we will reap the benefits and experience the blessings that come with perseverance. Paul writes that we ought to rejoice in our sufferings, for endurance "produces character, and character produces hope, and hope does not put us to shame, because God's love has been poured into our hearts through the Holy Spirit who has been given to us" (Rom. 5.5).

Here's the benefit of enduring: hope. It's an anchor that reminds us of His promises and His Spirit who is with us amidst our suffering, to strengthen and encourage us. Hope reminds us of His past, of the fact that He will make a way. He will move. He is here. Where despair kills all imagination, hope springs forth in vision and direction.

Cheyenne didn't allow her mind to fall so deeply into despair or dread that she lost the ability to imagine. Neither should we.

Let your trials motivate you further into His hope. Allow its peace to remind you that He hasn't failed you, nor will He.

Reflect on a time (past or present) dread or despair tried to diminish your imagination. How did God deliver you from that attack? How could the resolve to be creative in the midst of a trial affect your endurance?

Part Five

Anonymity

18

Challenge: Simple Callings

"Let her who bore you rejoice." – PROVERBS 23:25

There's a new simplicity awakened by motherhood. The late nights lingering in the nursing chair, gently cupping his face as I pray sweet futures over my baby. Late nights I used to spend wondering what my role is, what my purpose is, what I ought to be doing with my time.

That's been answered.

Simply mother. Simply love. One day at a time, one feeding cycle at a time, one diaper change at a time.

Time now begging to not be wasted or under appreciated. Time nudging me, reminding me that my purpose is here. In the now.

Might my mind and heart be present to absorb these sweet moments.

This role of motherhood — among the loving and nurturing — is to observe. The Lord is the day-by-day grower. My role is to capture these moments, snag and bottle them for a future day, possibly a rainy one where Graham needs to be reminded of who he is, how he's grown, where he's come from.

Despite sleep deprivation and a cup short of coffee, I open my eyes and stare at this teeny being. I jot down his peaked curiosity during bath time and finger holds during nursing and long, arched stretches after a good nap. I remember the baby smell, the sound of his cry, the smoothness of his cheeks and toes.

Observe. Take it in. This is where you're called to be, mama. Right here. In the quiet home, the drawn curtains, the anonymous season. Something is blossoming, don't you see it?

And in a world full of compromises and complications, remember the simplicity and power of your calling.

Mother.

And mother well.

Be present with your baby today. Write down what the Lord teaches and speaks to you through your time with him/her.

19

Lie: My Life is Insignificant

"In all things I have shown you that by working hard in this way we must help the weak and remember the words of the Lord Jesus, how he himself said, 'It is more blessed to give than to receive.'" – ACTS 20:35

It's 6 am. My baby's ready to start the day, screaming his head off for someone to come get him, and I've got the monitor on mute, a pillow over my head, covers over the pillow, and a prayer on repeat:

"Please, Lord, please let him sleep a little longer."

Nope.

My mind spins, tossing out the large list of things to do as I pick up my baby and start the day. All I can think about is sleep... coffee... silence.

When I finally put him down, I find myself sleeping, cleaning, cooking, doing laundry. All the fun things.

Then, a phone call with a friend who says, "Wow you must be so bored. What do you even do with your time?"

I try to figure out how to make chores, poopy diapers, loud screams, and sleep routines look like the cool-busy that a job - job is, but I'm left with the lie, "My life is insignificant."

Culture wants results on paper. Show me the Master's degree.

Show me your published pieces. Show me the rewards. Show me how you're successful.

And to culture, baby wipes and laundry detergent just don't cut it.

We feel hidden, and somehow ashamed of our inability to explain how our life is actually important. How our days are actually busier than one would think. How our bodies in these first few weeks require rest while we recover from delivery.

I'm here to tell you, dear mama, that you are more than your grocery store runs and laundry loads. You've got impact, the kind that doesn't have to be explained or validated by others. It's already seen by the Lord, and he says: your reward is great in Heaven. What better role than to disciple from day one?

Your child might not remember these first few days, your friends may not understand this new mom role, and you may never get any dollars or golden stars to tell you that you've done a good job, but remember that He is the God who sees.

He sees the things you do that no one else wants to do. He sees you taking care of someone who can't take care of themselves. He sees you offering love when there's none in return (just yet). He sees the lullabies and meals and clean home.

You are stewarding the things He's given you well, and "one who is faithful in a very little is also faithful in much" (Luke 16.10).

These hidden moments are brewing significant impact in culture. Be faithful and diligent in this season, and watch how the Lord uses it as preparation for the future.

What is the Lord teaching and speaking to you in this anonymous season?
List five, positive ways your new mom role is impacting your family.

20

Joy: Time's Fruit

"If it seems slow, wait for it: it will surely come: it will not delay." – HABAKKUK 2:3

I've got the happiest of babes this morning. I walked into his nursery, bent down over the crib and rubbed his head while whispering, "Good morning."

He threw out his arms in a long stretch, with the widest grin and little coo noise, as if to say "Good morning to you."

We spent most of our awake time playing on our tummies, something he typically protests. We talked to each other. I sang cheesy made-up songs with off melodies while he wiggled and cooed.

He gave a few faint yawns and I tucked him back in bed, rubbed his head while whispering, "Good night."

Off to sleep he went.

Let me tell you, dear mama, about the joy of time.

We spend the first few weeks trying to establish some sort of routine for our babies without any sort of response. We work hard at learning what's significant to our newborn and putting those things in place. We face the challenge of growing a baby and wonder, will this ever produce any fruit? Right now we don't see the outcome of our sowing and feel discouraged. But know that there's progress, there's growth leading to visible fruit just around the corner.

"If it seems slow, wait for it; it will surely come; it will not delay."

I kept waiting to see any evidence of Graham learning time, patience or routine. Would he ever agree to a wake time later than 5 or 6 am? A regular nap schedule?

Perhaps the Lord wants to grow those virtues we're trying to instill in our babies in us as well. He wants our patience as we teach patience to our babies. He asks for diligence and resilience through the tears and fits our infants throw at us. He knows that if we will not give up in these early weeks, we will witness what we've sown become fruit. We will partake in the joy of watching our babies learn the invaluable lessons time teaches.

We'll have the opportunity to wake our baby up, as he smiles and greets the day with his very own version of, "Good morning."

We'll watch him blossom among routine, as he learns there are different times and seasons for everything; there are tummy times and nap times and cuddle times and feeding times.

Wait for it. It'll come. Time is on our side.

What's tarrying, today? A consistent nap? A happy waketime?
Ask the Lord for patience while you wait for what you've implemented
to come into fruition.

21

Mary

THE SERVANT

"And blessed is she who believed that there would be a fulfillment of what was spoken to her from the Lord!" – LUKE 1:45

Meet Mary, who historians speculate was somewhere between 14 and 16 years old when visited by the angel Gabriel, who had a message. Mary found favor with God, and she would conceive a son to name Jesus. The son, THE Son. The Savior for all.

She doesn't understand. How will this be? I'm a virgin.

Gabriel reminds her, nothing is impossible with God. The Holy Spirit will work.

Forget your plans, Mary. Forget the dreams. Forget the reputation. You're about to have the responsibility of raising the perfect Son, the Messiah for all. No pressure.

Instead of responding with disbelief, with anger, or with fear, she says, "Behold, I am the servant of the Lord; let it be to me according to your word." (v. 38).

Wait.

Gabriel visits you, tells you that even though you're a virgin you're to bear a child, who happens to be God's Son.

Would you respond with, "Let it be to me according to your word?"

I'd probably be thinking, No one is going to believe this. Not my fiancé, my friends, my family. There goes my social media following, my career path, my dream guy.

But Mary says, "Behold, I am the servant of the Lord; let it be to me according to your word" (v. 38).

What strength. Her focus is set on His ways and not her own.

Certainly she faced challenges along the way. One can only imagine her journey. False shame and disdain from former friends. Misunderstood by society. The loneliness of no one being able to relate to her situation. Whether she recognized the impending challenges or not, she dismissed any justified or unjustified self-pity with, "I am the servant of the Lord."

Selfless, meek, and humble. Nevermind my plans, nevermind what other people will think. Your Word is true, and I am your servant.

Instead of focusing on herself, her shortcomings for the role or like-ability from neighbors, she decided to praise the Lord and trust Him amidst what was probably a lifelong season of anonymity.

"My soul magnifies the Lord, and my spirit rejoices in God my Savior...for behold, from now on all generations will call me blessed" (v. 46, 48).

Praise and divine wisdom for the future. She worshipped and magnified the Lord for what He would do while understanding her significant part, though hidden now, would indeed be blessed and remembered for all the generations to come. Might we position ourselves in the same manner, worshipping and magnifying the Lord for this significant role He's given us as mothers.

Let's not focus on the short goals. The small plans, the small perspective, the selfish self. Your role as a mom is part of a greater plan and bigger perspective. It extends past you into your family's future generations.

Let's praise Him for this unknown, often hidden, season. "For he who is mighty has done great things for me [yes, you!], and holy is his name" (v. 49).

Read Luke 1:26-38. Reflect on Mary's response to the angel. Where do you need to release control of your plans and say, "Let it be according to Your word?"

Part Six

Comparison

22

Challenge: Glancing Sideways

"But we have the mind of Christ." – 1 CORINTHIANS 2:16

"I will not reason and compare: my business is to create." - William Blake

I've been thinking a lot about this quote recently. How comparison leads to us being enslaved by the opinions of others. It strips us of creativity. It says, "this worked for this person so It must work for you."

Moms are experts on comparison. We like to think we're doing it better than the other mom (and vice versa). We like to validate the fact that our baby doesn't cry as much as theirs. We use it as an opportunity to feel superior. We judge the mom paving her own way, a way that looks different than how we do it.

They're not sticking to the status quo so they must be doing it wrong.

Or substitute they for we.

We often compare out of our own fears and insecurities. We don't want to stand out, to look different, to parent the unique way the Lord's designed us. So we modify and do what our mom friends tell us, afraid we'll look weird if we choose any unconventional routes.

I'd like to challenge us as women and mothers to stop comparing and start creating. He's given us the mind of Christ. Let's learn to think like Him, getting to know his thoughts and ideas before we morph and stifle our ideas for the sake of status quo.

Maybe this bathtub works for everyone else except your daughter. Maybe your sleep training methods look like a combination of a few rather than a total "CIO" method or "no cry solution." Maybe your bedtime routine, holiday traditions, or discipline system will look entirely different from any other family.

Good for you. Your business is to enter into the mind of Christ using your talents creatively. Your talents. Not your neighbor's.

Your baby needs all the fun combinations that make you *you*. Enter into that innovative place, where you can appreciate the unique makeup and ideas of other moms without comparing where God's called you and how He's made you.

Where do you find yourself comparing?
Where is He calling you to innovate?

23

Lie: She's Doing It Better

"She works with willing hands." – PROVERBS 31:13

One of the most common comparisons we make as new moms is of the stay-at-home vs. working mom.

Oftentimes, the stay-at-home mom is considered irrelevant to society. "She must be incredibly bored with so little to do." More often than not people don't see it as a job. It looks lazy compared to those other moms who do it all.

The only questions we stay-at-home moms ever really get are, "So when are you going back to work?"

Society values the big bucks. The career with the Banana Republic outfit.

We all know stay-at-home moms don't gain revenue by watching their kids or tending to their home (unless you're Insta famous and companies pay you to put your baby in their clothes with your very own exclusive discount code). So instead of appreciating the important role they play in raising up a child in the way they should go (Prov. 22.6), they're disregarded as worthless.

Now, onto the working mom.

The stay-at-home moms glower. They think, you care more about your income than your child. "I would never let my kid be raised in a daycare."

There's the judgmental warnings of your baby getting more sick, you not being present in your baby's life, you not prioritizing your home.

Your single, childless coworkers don't understand the different hats of career, mother, etc. Neither do your stay-at-home mom friends.

It's time for us to stop comparing, judging, or analyzing who has it better, and start asking the Lord where He's calling us.

What are your family's needs?

Is it a presence in the home? Someone to cook, clean, garden? Does your baby need you there with him/her?

Or does your family need additional income? Does your household need you to help provide for that pack of diapers, that electricity bill, that mortgage?

It's time we stop considering what society deems valuable vs. worthless, or what women say is protecting a child vs. neglecting a child. Start considering your family's needs, and where the Lord wants you.

"She works with willing hands" looks like different things in different seasons. It can mean lawn work outside your home. Sowing a dress for your daughter. Typing up copy for the magazine. Teaching a class at the local middle school.

She *works*.

Where the Lord is calling you, go. Work. We aren't called to be idle. He fashioned us for work, whether that's in our home loving on our babies or at an office building making money and still loving on our babies.

She works with *willing hands*.

You must be willing. If it's a job, be present. If it's at home, be present. Don't waste your hours wishing you were somewhere else, wondering if she has it better. If you're where He's calling you for this season, then be all in. Be willing to let Him show you and carry you through the lessons and trials and victories.

Like Solomon writes, "Give her [the woman who fears the Lord] of the fruit of her hands, and let her works praise her in the gates" (Prov. 31.31).

Where are you right now? Home? Working?
Wherever it is, are you working with willing hands?
What changes do you need to make to be all in?

24

Joy: Comparison vs. Collaboration

"And let us consider how to stir up one another to love and good works, not neglecting to meet together, as is the habit of some..."
– HEBREWS 10:24-25

I think most of us are afraid of admitting we don't know. Especially as mothers. Shouldn't we know by now why our infant or child is upset? Don't we have the solution?

People ask how we are, and we tuck our answers away, zip-locked in isolation while we respond, "very good, thank you." We respond with certainty, when we often feel helpless. We pretend it's easy, because after all, staying at home doing "nothing" all day should be simple. Right? It's those hardworking women who really have the challenge. I mean, it's easy to extend grace to those moms while showering disdain over the moms at home still trying to figure this new role out.

But this is what I've learned about motherhood. There's a rather large community surrounding it. Imperfect, sure. Full of differing opinions, certainly. But if we'd just ask for help, if we'd merely admit what we don't know instead of worrying how that may come across, perhaps we'd learn from those "old-fashioned" generations who made a way without video monitors and high tech strollers and the Google search bar.

I'm pretty sure I've called my mom at least three times a day. Is it normal for my little one to sweat? How do get him to fall asleep without us both crying? Can I stroll him in the freezing cold?

Every mother has and develops that ambiguous but true sense, "mother's intuition." But dear momma, do not forget the 85.4 million mothers residing here in the US. They're realizing their ignorance and seeking answers just like you. You're not alone!

There are so many women who have been (and are in your shoes — there's no excuse for mothering alone. Stroll dates, FaceTimes, run-ins at the grocery store....

Let's be real with our struggles and open with what's worked and failed along this incredible and sometimes exhausting journey. Someone out there needs to hear your experience, and all mothers need your grace.

> *Where's your community right now? Does that circle need to expand? Ask the Lord for a few names of people missing in your inner circle. Be bold and reach out to those women.*

25

Abigail Adams

THE CHALLENGER

"Let us not love in word or talk but in deed and in truth." – 1 JOHN 3:18

Meet Abigail Adams, the First Lady of America's second president. She aspired to a better future for women, formulating her own opinions on matters that most women wouldn't dare consider back in the 1700's. For example, she was against slavery and in favor of women's education. Though she had no formal education herself, she "availed herself of the family's library to master subjects most women never considered."[1]

I love her boldness and outspokenness revealed throughout her letters to her Harvard graduate of a husband.

She said things like,

"You need not be told how much female education is neglected, nor how fashionable it has been to ridicule female learning."[2]

And,

"I desire you would Remember the Ladies, and be more generous and favourable to them than your ancestors … Remember all Men would be tyrants if they could.

If particular attention is not paid to the Ladies we are determined to foment a Rebellion, and will not hold ourselves bound by any Laws in which we have no Voice, or Representation."[3]

She did not neglect her family to pursue these rights. She managed their family's farm and business affairs, making successful investment decisions on behalf of her family.[4] This was almost unheard of at the time, considering most married women had limitations on their property rights. She did this while supporting her husband's career and raising their children.

Abigail embodies the William Blake quote we discussed: "I will not reason and compare: my business is to create."

She didn't compare her voice to women of the past, nor did she assume what has been will be. Instead, she sparked conversation with the unfavorable truth. Women have rights. Women can manage. Moms have "a vital role in preparing sons to be virtuous citizens and leaders in the new republic."[5]

You have a voice, mama. Do not neglect to use it. Speak truth and share it boldly. If we're intentional and committed, we can impact society without compromising our role at home.

Prayerfully consider where the Lord may be calling you to be bold and use your voice to speak truth into society. How can you balance impacting culture with being present in the home?

Part Seven
Culture

26

Challenge: Inconvenienced

"Behold, children are a heritage from the Lord, the fruit of the womb a reward. Like arrows in the hand of a warrior are the children[a] of one's youth. Blessed is the man who fills his quiver with them! He shall not be put to shame when he speaks with his enemies in the gate."

– PSALM 127:3-5

Children are a blessing.

I'm sure we've heard this before, possibly recently, but culture doesn't seem to understand this.

In our first month of marriage, so many men and women, young and old, told me and my husband things like, "Spend this time just enjoying being alone." Or, "Travel now, while you can…" Or, "It's best to really launch into your career for a few years before having kids."

Delay, delay, delay.

Never mind what the Lord may want. Don't ask, don't consider. You're 22. You're too young.

Of course, no one blatantly came out and said, "Children are a burden, a hindrance, a permanent hitch in your dreams."

But there's an underlying attitude that acts as if it's more responsible and mature to wait and have kids as opposed to having them as soon as you get married.

Not one person encouraged me to have kids immediately. In fact, everyone we talked to discouraged it.

It wasn't like my husband and I were ready, whatever *ready* means. But the Lord kept telling us to trust Him and release control in all aspects of our life, including this. We believed that meant babies years down the line, but two months later, bam. Three sticks that read "positive."

Maybe you waited years and planned. Maybe you're like me and had your own plans, but the Lord overrode those. Either way, you've got a baby now, and rather than seeing that as an inconvenience, we as moms need to understand the implications of Psalm 127:3-5. If children are a heritage from the Lord, as the Word says, and a tremendous blessing from Him, then we are called to cherish that gift in obedience and thankfulness. It means He's given you the responsibility for discipling, protecting, loving, and serving your infant.

We must begin to live in agreement with His Word, living out the fact that our babies are a reward and a blessing to us, by the way we speak to and about them, how we live sacrificially, and in our general attitude towards them.

"Your eyes saw my unformed substance; in your book were written, every one of them, the days that were formed for me, when as yet there was none of them" (Ps. 139.16).

It's no accident your baby's here. Right now. There's purpose in his/her arrival. Don't let culture tell you this baby is an impediment to your future. Remember, your little arrow will be a defense and a protection for your family in the years to come.

As you hold your baby, remember you are holding a tangible, living blessing from the Lord. Treat it as such, and watch the blessing grow and multiply with time.

Spend time praising and thanking the Lord today for His wonderful gift of life. Thank Him for including you with such a large, powerful blessing.

27

Lie: I Need To Be In Control

"Truly you are the Son of God!" – MATTHEW 14:33

"Nothing comes to you without passing His fingers first."

This morning I knew it was time to write about control, but felt helpless at where to start. Do I write about how Graham slept through the night for the first time last night, as if I controlled that? Or how while we can't control our babies, with a disciplined schedule we can help better manage their days? Do I write about my fear of taking him out in public and causing a scene? How, if I'm being honest, most days are fairly unpredictable and I hate not having more control?

Instead, I heard, "Matthew."

I flipped my mom's Bible open to a random spot in Matthew and started reading.

It was the passage where Jesus walks on water, then Peter follows, until he sees the wind and fears.

I glanced at my mom's notes from her own quiet times and various church sermons.

First, "Nothing comes to you without passing His fingers first."

And then, "The disciples were in the perfect will of God and also in the perfect storm."

"Obeying God can sometimes lead to rough sailing."

This is good, I thought. I felt Him telling me to keep reading.

"Out of control and Jesus put you here."

Ah.

How often I have acted like I've got this motherhood thing under control. How guilty I have felt when I failed. There are so many apps out there that tell us if we do these things, our baby will sleep better or walk faster. And maybe those things are true. But let's face it. There are hours where our baby cries for no reason. There are nights they sleep horribly. We like to reason, to explain away, as if we know. Or we fall into the trap of feeling guilty, thinking, "I must not be doing something right." But we don't need to know, because He does.

I think the Lord's placed you and me here, in this position as new moms, to remind us that Jesus has us in this perfect storm for a reason. The will of God brought you to this place so that you'd discover who He is. At the end of the story, the disciples said, "Truly you are the Son of God" (Matt. 14:33). May we face these storms without control, under His, and say with His disciples, "Ah, yes, truly You are Lord!"

Let's use these moments that are out of our hands to watch what He does. Watch how He provides for you and your baby. Let Him show you He is Lord of all. He's amidst everything you're experiencing and feeling.

Take comfort in the fact that "nothing comes to you without passing His fingers first."

What storm are you battling today? Where do you feel totally out-of-control? What is Jesus teaching you about Himself?

28

Joy: Undignified Worship

"They rejoiced with exceedingly great joy." – MATTHEW 2:10

I love watching Graham stare in wonder at my made-up songs.

Sometimes it seems as if he's cooing along to them. I'll sing "I loooovvvveeee yoooouuuu" in the most exaggerated, pitchy voice. No judgment. No annoyance. Just a mouth opening up into an o-shape, forming the widest of smiles.

His pleasant demeanor has me thinking about our significant influence in how our little ones worship.

When the Magi saw Jesus as a toddler, they rejoiced with "exceedingly great joy."

We entertain our babies with dramatic hand gestures, catchy beats, and funny voice inflections.

But talk about spiritual things and suddenly that disappears. So often we maintain a stiff posture when we approach His throne, and our kids see that. They notice your arms flailing and feet tapping at home. They learn the "church stance" during service — the hands down, head down, voice low.

They mimic you.

They discover through your actions that church is where you dress up and stand still, while home is the place you can really be yourself and let loose.

The nursery rhymes are fun. Worship isn't. Worship is serious business.

Let me ask: How do you worship? What example are you setting for your baby with how you worship Jesus?

We can help our babies discover the exceedingly great joy that comes with knowing and seeing Jesus. Joy that produces a heart of worship, with abandoned hands and the widest of smiles. It starts with us and how we choose to praise Him.

Worship doesn't demand the right lyrics, beat, or voice. It requires a surrendered, thankful you. Thankfulness from the heart. An unashamed voice.

We have the authority to show our babies the power of worship and the wonder of knowing our Father. Right now. In our homes. In the quiet lullabies to sleep and tummy times and nightly baths.

There's no judgment. No annoyance. No dignity even. Just the Lord's mouth opening up into an o-shape, forming the widest of smiles.

Answer the following questions mentioned earlier: How do you worship? What example are you setting for your baby with how you worship Jesus? Read 2 Samuel 6:16-23 to see a heart well-postured in worship.

29

Barbara Bush

THE INFLUENCER

"And these words that I command you today shall be on your heart. You shall teach
them diligently to your children, and shall talk of them when you sit in your house,
and when you walk by the way, and when you lie down, and when you rise."

– DEUTERONOMY 6:6-7

Meet Barbara Bush.

"The wife, mother, grandmother, military spouse, and former First Lady...an advocate of the American family."[1]

She's an example of what it looks like to impact culture without compromising family.

She embodied flexibility, moving 29 times for the sake of her husband and family.

She started the Barbara Bush Foundation for Family Literacy, which has raised over $110 million for literary programs across America.

She also visited Grandma's House, a residential care home for children with HIV/AIDS. There's a famous photo of her holding an infant infected with AIDS on her shoulder, as if to encourage the public to extend a hand to those we deem "untouchable."

Amidst her influence in numerous presidential campaigns, her hard work to fight illiteracy and HIV/AIDS, and even her authoring a children's book, Barbara knew her most important role was in the home. She recognized the bedrock of our nation's stability is the family and that its age-old principles must remain in tact.

Let her words encourage you in your new role:

"We are in a transitional period right now – fascinating and exhilarating times, learning to adjust to the change and the choices we, men and women, are facing. Maybe we should adjust faster, maybe slower. But whatever the era, whatever the times, one thing will never change. Fathers and mothers, if you have children, they must come first. You must read to your children, and you must hug your children, and you must love your children. Your success as a family, our success as a society, depends not on what happens in the White House, but on what happens in your house."[2]

Reread this quote. What does success look like to you? How can you achieve that in your household?

Reflection

"Examine yourselves, to see whether you are in the faith." – 2 CORINTHIANS 13:5

One whole month.

It's hard to believe, to reconcile the long days with how quickly the weeks passed. I'm certain we've experienced every emotion possible in the process.

Take a look at your baby now. What things has he/she overcome?

Since beginning this devo, Graham has mastered the art of steady eye contact and conversation. He's transitioned fully to his crib. He's outgrown my favorite swaddle. He likes music. He's social. He still cries, but he sure can throw a wide grin that'll melt the coldest of hearts. I've witnessed a steadiness, a peace, and an energy that keeps growing with each passing day.

Now you. What are your breakthroughs? Write down a few. Reflect on the victories, large and small, from the past month. What things has He spoken to you? What Scripture verses have been an encouragement? How have you grown? What season are you in, and where's His Spirit leading you? What's the greatest laugh you've had?

Spend one day each month journaling your responses to these questions. Watch the little and large milestones unravel with time. As you look back through your journal, you will discover His attentiveness to your family's needs, His faithfulness over all things, and His radical love that consistently matures and purifies. Someday, you can show your little one these monthly reflections of breakthrough and answered prayers. Perhaps He will use our testimonies to encourage our children in their walks, too.

Acknowledgments

Behind every book and every author is a team of people inspiring, encouraging, designing, and challenging. A special thanks to my spectacular team, who without their wisdom and talent this devotional would have far too many misplaced commas, cringey clichés, and dull pages.

Margo— Thank you for your artistic mind that somehow knew exactly what this devo needed. Your visionary touch breathes life and vibrancy into the words on these pages. I couldn't have done it without you.

All the ladies I interviewed and highlighted for this devotional — especially Robin, Cheyenne, and my mom — thank you. Thank you for your vulnerability that will touch the lives of other moms across the globe. Your stories have forever changed me.

Misty Gallo— A special thanks for your keen eyes. From high school history papers till now, I've always appreciated your edits.

Uncle Carl— Thank you for your encouragement in writing this book. It would've never been published without your knowledge on how to do so.

And finally, John Tyler— No words or expression of gratitude will put to justice just exactly how present and wonderful you've been throughout the highs and lows of writing a book. From editing past midnight to holding our crying baby while I jot down my ideas, your delight towards me pursuing my dreams just about brings me to tears. I love you.

Bibliography

Intro into Motherhood:

Holy Bible: English Standard Version. Crossway Bibles, 2001.

From Darkness to Light:

The Bible: The New King James Version. T. Nelson, 1984.

Meyer, Joyce. *Power Thoughts Devotional: 365 Daily Inspirations for Winning the Battle of Your Mind.* Hodder, 2014.

Lie: I'm the Only One

Holy Bible: English Standard Version. Crossway Bibles, 2001.

Robin Barlow: The Heavenly Thinker

Tutkaluk, Ally. "Richters Syndrome." *Leukaemia Foundation,* 18 June 2019, https://www.leukaemia.org.au/disease-information/leukaemias/chronic-lymphocytic-leukaemia/richters-syndrome/.

Abigail Adams: The Challenger

1. Michals, Debra. "Abigail Smith Adams." *National Women's History Museum,* 2015, https://www.womenshistory.org/education-resources/biographies/abigail-adams.

2. & 3. Adams, Charles Francis. *Familiar Letters of John Adams and His Wife*

Abigail Adams, During the Revolution: With a Memoir of Mrs. Adams (Classic Reprint). Hurd and Houghton, 1876.

4. Holton, Woody. "Abigail Adams, Bond Speculator." *The William and Mary Quarterly,* vol. 64, no. 4, 2007, pp. 821–838. JSTOR, www.jstor.org/stable/25096751.

5. Michals, Debra. "Abigail Smith Adams." *National Women's History Museum,* 2015, https://www.womenshistory.org/education-resources/biographies/abigail-adams.

Barbara Bush: The Influencer

1. Trump, Donald. "Statement from the President on the Passing of Former First Lady Barbara Bush." *The White House,* The United States Government, 17 Apr. 2018, https://www.whitehouse.gov/briefings-statements/statement-president-passing-former-first-lady-barbara-bush/. Transcript.

2. Bush, Barbara. "Mrs. Bush's Commencement Address to the Wellesley College Class of 1990." Wellesley, MA.

Notes

Notes

Notes

Notes

Notes

Notes

Notes

Made in the USA
Coppell, TX
13 February 2020